Silent Street

Other prose-poetry by Marc Atkins

The Logic of the Stairwell, and Other Images (Shearsman)
The Prism Walls (Contraband)

Marc Atkins

Silent Street

Shearsman Books

First published in the United Kingdom in 2018 by
Shearsman Books
50 Westons Hill Drive
Emersons Green
BRISTOL
BS16 7DF

Shearsman Books Ltd Registered Office
30–31 St. James Place, Mangotsfield, Bristol BS16 9JB
(this address not for correspondence)

www.shearsman.com

ISBN 978-1-84861-570-0

Contents

WHtBJ	11
All Cease	12
Unhung Gates	13
Woken Breed	14
Well Keeped	15
Today	16
Third's Person	17
Broken Pewter	18
Cellular	19
From Here Amongst the Useless Worthlessness Has Credit	20
Thousands Degree Shade	27
Lineless	28
INgrain	30
Ausländer	33
The End of Suicide	34
Unrest	38
Silent Street	39
Rattle's Alley	40
Sentinel	43
Pleasantly Imbalanced	44
Over Western Docks	45
Night Train from Liège	47
Shutting Down	48
Iota	49
Marianne Moore is the Girl with the Pearl Earring	50
Edges	51
Insanitary Bite	52
If I Wake Then What Shall I Do	53
Waive	54
Fourth Night	55
For Méliès	56

Parasite Paradise	57
Roadside	58
Distant Absence	60
Dilation	61
Dark Under Sunrise	62
Tyranny	63
Paper Day	64
Blank	65
Street Grain	66
Stop Minding Lots	67
Landscape	68
Calafon	69
Beside the Wall	71
The Carcass of an Insufficient	72
Height of a Postbox	74
South of Autumn	76
The Institute of Incoherent Geography	77
Scuff Marks	79
Passing on	81
Discoloured	82

For Lola

Silent Street

WHtBJ

Calling, remote, cresting breaths gradually flake across a bated line of silent paternoster fibulae, a blanched name encrusted, branch failed entrusted, tallied by grappling with a pavement of out folds, unfocused as reversing trams, weathered in fornicating light, stark by numeric exposure, recordings from a nipped finger, flapped digital, unhurried dialling, connubial concertina, flicked along from band F aggression, fading from winnowing light, up before D, darkness falls once and never, amore, carried into the mistimed hole, mistletoe for the unrhymed cranny, beaten by papered feet, the calling hardly stops, venture tallow, standard cranial, ripping anonyms, wire to wire shell-like, an O in for each corner, suns on skins, rip through rivets, bleating others wait now amongst ocean wilds, skipping on sands until sucked to the core, spume rains on the immature, the bleak past wastes a good view and eye-liner straight rivers always bend a little, barely missed call weighting, green from new, a bursting chill seeps in from the darker side of weaving rocks, welled deep, colour coded crevice, stopped cocks, spines like books, read in those bitter hours, films happening to infants, odd voices tiring, worn by past tongues, roads threading, this, another arbitrary notation, sharp beams, insufficient edges, untimely grazes, and each waits inelegantly for unspannable arches to creak, then grit by grit sooner and longer to fall.

All Cease

Eye crawl virtual intolerance beading corners crease dread blinks white lather squeals cracks recent hear un un un repellent leaking twists grating trails slime slavered ingenious engrossed sucking lip pits mouth crowded grout dusty stockings nailed past floor board simpering blessed crazed nothing enough board puritan put crest crowded bestial meat int o full grit soft pallor scratch small touches little flag st one mote pick-panic eating eating eatin eati at ei atop nn soup slid corner cracks un unnoticed mark with out o place enough dribble in in cornerstone calumny open insi der brakes across twelve fingered dust with in an other h and a slip cull c sharper trinket plumes s unny death day save incident said e did in a solemn pillar twists weigh weight wrestle killed creel croat under waste supper stand all mark ed lines un recon diti oned weathered within her e an d he re struggle ing drainin g smile ing work fair world in crease will ing walk ing end ear th's sodium light concrete wher e we found sea e scape suns sit blank scant horizonn small hands pawing rain great grease holdd inspections jerked night c rawls over label mark nneutral oration pleased Quai d'Orsay ridicule semblance's too ultradian u u un voiced with.

Unhung Gates

Groups gather about unhung gates, debating necessary applications of orders contrarious, largely of immaterial nature, from which to draw appropriate determination, transgressions which each distinct impropriators had unwittingly or otherwise disgraced a generally unassailable, irrefutable street. Beneath a clutching of enquiring notes, dripping fervid of palimpsestory ink, lay a key for which each much bodied gatherer pored over many a generational year, its fathoming being sole purpose for collected aspirational coterie, indeed clustering was the only apposite force over which to hover cohesive eye. So waited, daydream chatted, unburdened by enthusiasm, codes fail disentanglement fall from minds as bugs from peccant blanket. Trammels scarcely abated, prolixity of intemperate good-nights weighed unfathomably upon scattering clattering progression to crumbling doors of ill-lit ill disposed abodes.

Woken Breed

Moment murmured alights as doors peel open and all presentiments hiding stage right fall into this withdrawing room. Irregular suns drift, peer-glass, pecked walls, ancillary floors, fluxus body, bandaged calm air, invisible indivisible figures astride, forming first gaseous perturbation, wireless incantation, bruised walls uncleaned by virtue, visitors pupating in carriages, crack a little, each upheaves scene to floor-less levels. Signs then doors, each creaking ascend, sign then doors, carriages do not stop at signs, signs then door, whirring wiring waring clatter, sign then door, paper scatter cooling fans, whirrs and doors, signs and scatters. Crawling floor where horses run, wires dry, ropes knot, or alternative, proxy plays out, pays out, caress carcass door, take stop Discontinue, turn watch not watchers, door then sign, ascend and doors, past shadowers, hiders from habitual watchers, signs on each closing door, those naked wait beside turners' gate, fearing under-step, mark by mark, to here from here, step not steep, recollections be other rooms, wait beside one unwatered bed, curtained walls, sunless fall from bud to bud, down to down, milestones clap hands, at each bend, taps and murmurs, trailing sheets, bodies twitch, cacographic wires snap rap on unchaste walls, and this last warp of cloistered doors, each in turn, close to.

Well Keeped

Scantlings keeped well, cradling fine sandy soup, sludged fortunate glazed, starer panoramic erased, parch overcome, dug drudge during tipping hour, pall stage, pallid sage, weather'd crocks creasing, inapparent rocks retching, gagging snug, hid from bails of rain, brackish dribble, wincing grapple, curd fools-ware, pinch fallow, demonising table, mediaevaled rooms, settlers swipe fallacies into mouths, Hypnos fissuring, cast running, furlong and chain, flail grasping, gasping spawn, sunny crimes, hanged leaden bricks, drawn breadth, inhale light, noose height, inner working merchant's dip, shot hardened, rail trailed, Caliban froth, incessant laps, fur knifes, long train grain trail, tail mouths haul slipshod, listing tow avowing up- and-crawling seas, aniseed duly rushing drank, napkin immaculate, impostors boo, imposing roofs, vane rust, wincing sonnets, coy ballets caw-cawing, conspiracy dust, dogs plight, bleary orthology, medley ahh, moonspit petal-donna, ampere blather, marionette white, fluff hides, cold sawing, swept corrosion, crania-crania, pull-peasants porch, full whither, balloon squeal, eloquent equal, chair laces, cutaway spray, spell dripping, spoken footsteps, shushed innocent, inking spills, posing cricks, unsettled impostures, dust-sheet imposter, floor bursts, open warp, media whistles, formerly assigned gin tunnel, a final fall-short, shot-felled, balm chilled, room wasting, scrying trinkets, all-ended rasping, preferential mistresses, sun over sigh, dimensions pre-scripted.

Today

Today is a day of streets, uneven entangled, propagating cobbles, damp from bleedin' feet, lips bi-dry over lay wasted ways, everyday hours' calm despair, pasty hands, naillessness hand-holds, finger skipping, ever starving, marchioness grilling, parasites calling, bridges befalling, dripping yellow ancestors, waist fording rillets, plaster grown fields, palsic crows carrying, stung by bats, wetted by cuts, hands barbed passed softened pillows, climbed across this bed of tallow, to hollowed hills, disentangled shallows, a meadow of conversation, suffocating coherence, untied by granulated history of indifference, a mucid sun leaks into the wanderer, inspissated moon, gurgling towers, girdled cargo stops, propped along that venerable aqueduct, light water gathered beneath burning arches, boat workers holding, two to a billhook, fucking lacemakers on suicide bridge, unhurriedly gleaning implausible relics floating voice-like out across interlacing veils.

Third's Person

Easily engorged figurines walk beside lacerated characters, vaults of incoherent images hide behind shelves of silvered self-absorbing jars, glancing distant hostel lights, deformed expressions lit from below by exhausted flames of gravel scented cierge. Here where fingers meet, expeditious eyes see round corners, she bends to distortions woven in massed hands, stepping from vent to vent, standing aside from those huddled, eating as they play, with backs to their crumbling road and ill-met feet buried, an approved medium, sand, dirt or loam, illustrating squat columns on any edge of her paper, bleeding margins being cornered by de-sanitised sanctimones. Now as then, relentless national assassins talk only to themselves, beating frost from magnified faces, as other figures, who haemorrhage freely from their tongues, talk reflectively to glassy floors, outside that failing fence, scourged waves and combustible crania edge its bourne, attempting rebirth, miss their mouths and lie quietly manducating a tedious grey, leaden scenting oiling air, whispering to other rooms, where an exhibition is misplaced behind all its little doors, numbered expressions peel from a scratched waxed coating, just audible, dribbling naked feet waste away floors of dead-end corridors, so laid toe by toe, a memory for everything, Jalsaghar doormen scurry for their final horse ride, on Geometers' Island many whale tailored folds bleat from neck-up ties, auto-derision spreading between courses, a fogging of fine dancers, coda, calls silence on a music-less room.

Broken Pewter

Powdery fog bleached the underwings of greasy stone demons, alongside, uncropped figures stand marmoreal-like under ebbing leaves of slobbering trees, cracked and crazed, a putrefying mist settles across the slickie ground, masking indecipherable a blanched table of crazed crocks and jellied tea.

Instrumental to amercing that pungent aspect were grazing windmills of undimensional form, plucked, pickled and entangled by darkling birds line pegged between shimmering alain poles, a suspension no, a suspect of learning, a desaturated lull, sampling fleet undulates, indivisible voices taped over recoiling ears, fallen amongst impenetrable melodies and disgustful vegetation.

On pity's stone bench I wrote of unsprung rats, ruth lenses lamenting felled gleaning dust, shredded figures lying curled amongst desert paper, ink-less pens vomiting over poor eclair's simpering cassock, or hassock, or wassock, fatty glazed windowless streets reflect a flagging perspective, widowed lamps whistling across a lying stream of unopened lips, thigh high tapes of stammering answer machine recordings, tattered spools of Murnau, a pencilled number of Madeline alone, coin shod at Wayland's Smithy, ripped clock-out cards spat at tapped walls, close-up sheepish particles, unwrapped Faust shouts in a sand garden, La Gioconda lens blurred mirror doors of a room yet built, sitting in a whiskey glass silting cuffs, a plane pen winging Lumière over a fading page began neolithic writing, settling on flecked graphene, accounting for this last of an unsure day.

Cellular

I once tried to exchange my books for a blanket with the man who lived upstairs, he refused. Thoughts dry across skin, where memories dismantle with age, disenthralling us from an unrecognisable past, an unclaimable past, I no longer know to whom I write, saints tied gunpowder to recusant legs, semi-dressed and circumspect, when do mornings stop, hours and wolves rain on the roofs, waiting for no particular date, first wet light glancing an unpeopled street, dull blades overcast corked letters, steaming ink reflecting antecedes hiding in a hollow of shadowed buildings, there this Village, where was never glid before, myriad ways and countless zones now ossified by unclean voices. It is worth living through a year just for a single Autumn day.

From Here Amongst the Useless Worthlessness Has Credit

Crawling from vivid lakes of cracked glass, ripped skins of pleading metamorphs bind their anxious hands. Along holloways figures form, mimicking thirsty sleep, pale fingers following along, by line by line, by step by step, an Alartum Illustratus, containing noted, denuded and engorged over-drawn engravings, burdened ineluctability in a tyranny of logic, unsystematic schema, progressed abscess, first steps towards, positioning fact, facilitated bedlam, surety fields, customary obligatory, corresponding to conviction. Second, beyond Bayeux, held dripping, adjacent retch, statement arrangement fitting squarely into a Straining Machine, draughty eyed unsurety, trans-positioning intention. Third, insufficiently oxygenated step, conceived misstep, momentary hypo-wondering, lost disposition, virtually pallid, between avowed and exiguous vertigo. Fourth, securely overseen, adventures in reverie, dissatisfied necessity, moving from unravelled ladders, affecting gables, treasonous asides, venture a toe to the splintered floor, bi-line undertaking, waxing curious, counter-conditional. Fifth, exhaustion snapping, flapp-p-p-p-ping spool, mouth of moss, month of moths, impossible execution, wonted in-step, dot, dot, dot. Eighth, irreverent, playing irrelevance, attacking no sense clause, see section C, thoroughly unsmiling, backing unhurriedly towards a cornered room. Ninth, derelict rage, spoken mechanically calm, intimate tone specifications, reject forgetting, lessening distance, longer biting knots. Tenth, step lined, instinct simpatic-o, indistinct automatic, cow blather, teething purple, purposely aim, objectified welling, standing mnemonic, unreasoned race, bait between, uneven selves. Eleventh, auto-belief, borax regimen, click projection, clack protection, looming split, raged stillness, charged necessity, over screaming, whim counting, drops of saline, splash grain, entangled cloud lines, grinding power, grime signs wake cooling sepia scars.

From here amongst the useless, worthlessness has credit, plane strip, draping rain sweat, unhazardous bodies, reaping sweet, aleatory inveterates, sedating box, ex-mandate, straight bore, overtly stable, nascent leaks, proposition vitriol, twice unpicked, contrail entanglement, unsmoked kale, open scale, fibrous hail, duty post-sacred, annotated scar lines, plaited decadent, homicidal wasteland, stretching inequity, pronounced unnecessary, work-houses redefined defiance, unnecessary other, mother dutiful fiction, projectable outcome, within mass, oblate obvious solitude. Next step, cuts doubt, born coupling, past about past, declaration emphasis, ideas brush, born putrid, become crystal, purity friction, vandal fictions, point on being on point. Naked lie lines, function on history, silence signified, saintly scratchings, sum of torture, mythologies of prospect, visitant trailer made, tolerantly calm, wondering would sell, dreams for mortality, loosening grips a visionary, symbolic tracts, enabling rips, wary of drips, confuse need with waste, placing each finger at each margin, be a fork on the wayside, I sat without a shadow, evade to ring, evidence of spilling, towering sap, imitation names, pleasure cracks, a charity of demons, with gifts of indifference, effervescent fiends, awaken cold, unfettered geld, disbursed amongst carrion clouds. There besides, words we wish to in-habit, lesser blood seeped from whorl of her small fingers, an eventual sky, darken and unnecessary, anti-century sounds fade from a frozen radio. Sharp noised, unbroken bedlam, unpardonable by pages, intimidation slept, with tongues between teeth, enough was one word once, sounds wetted her fingers, trail close, unlaced stones, running images, stolen by gesture, coloured in morning, covered on amounts, paper stains, miming ferryman, thought dust, saline pockets, dried last, at the end of an unfound Autumn. Days loose, grit based, over filmed, con race, seep remanence, pictures pasted behind peeling posters, too few remember, lights of this long road, following her eyes, where chalk statues sat, they tell each to each dismantled stories, read from pages torn from books.

Corroded corridors, high ceilinged rooms interleaved, speaker voices overlap, crowd mould, imposition images, fleshed-out island, figured looking, window faced, other missed, imagining done, wander into a sea, dusted by sunsets, woken by footprints, wait on bleached chairs, bemothed moons oil indefinite lakes, lie on malleable mountain, metering sunsets, counting dispassion, tamed tapping, suspicion arrives, breezing willows, soluble narrative, fallacious Wulfila, pupil drying enlightenment.

Here is where rot stumbles, thorn weight forest, frosted rough-cut trees, stuttering plank shadows, sitting beside vast sweeping hillside, she tore words nesting amongst snowy graves, she threw words of canned confessional, islets through which are seen irreal watchmen, impatient crowds, stand out amongst hurrying brides, wringing pores, threadbare ropes, releasing tides, entangling days, cries calling traitors, passing barricades, dogstenched alleyways, unhinged claps, over-sung rasps, repeat in fogging mirrors, repellent minors bleed with religious skincare, clarifying hardware, rumoured steps give way to razors, over tightening lay waste unbuilt towers, little shading an undrained desert, brick-lined shadows, watching executioners stand beside failure, tearfully overhearing a catcher's lie.

Depression as a form of boredom, waiting rooms as null field space, seeping wordlessness, fields of shallow antonyms, pitched voices close around temporal boxes on which we sit, scrape back felt snow from a second box of free dimensions, rising now, pull back, a third box, a fourth, fifth, an endless field of boxes lining as a disposition of dust, on to a transparent horizon.

Clothed red she waits in a far green field, mechanical mists perpetually reforming lie alone, a wearing gate, a mortal cry drifting across this whiter land, echoing in her pale mouth, catching seeds on the peeling air, she divagates into my thoughts, once more for the last time.

Two cities, where one was read, of people who stand on bridges, walk towards buildings, hesitate, deviate, cross and uncross shallow pavements, reflect on bleating ideas, consider where to wait, clamour for sounds, wash in echoes, throw words at windows, pass notions through glass into a world of concrete towers and diseased trees, across many empty streets, where footsteps recapitulate before corners, lost in distance, confessed by suspicion, an unknown who follows, documents, maps archives, a thing to do, a sole matter of a life's work. Death doesn't recognise veiled faces, misunderstood intentions are only tragedy, missed thoughts flattened by hand, discredited and pinned as hollow-hearted parchment, corrupted senses bleeding through notional matter, uncloaked definitions, unsold aberrations, tragic forms, abhorrent information, indifference drives voyager, indecipherable brays behind every unfathomable door, four caliginous steps, through worthy cracks, murmuring freeze, an unrequited breeze, enticed air, other bodies' heat, visible through mist, latched mouths line beneath dripping ringing stalactites, turning a wheelless road, resting on echoes, climbing by oarsmen's strokes, longing a deserted hithe, feet fading, lampposts pooling huddled strangers, grime-light breaching each small room, breathing greedily stagnant, air where lingering inhabitants turn from windows, walk in shallow light of unused mornings.

I stepped from an unstarred boat and stood aimless on a rotting dock, sea ground about that island, lazily dismantling its sweltering form, an only path distanced itself before me, effortlessly yielding to an unwarm sun and unenthusiastically coloured land. Through wondering hours I navigated a yellowing land, breaching barriers, enthusing at verticals, losing horizons, until I followed no path leading to a sea, I am tired of screaming, drawn towards and prevented from going nowhere, April is an unknown month, only in April is anyone alone, silence hammers at my head, until a day, a quiet day, an unachieved day.

Horizon of rivers, swollen departure, valleys dismembered, ideation archaeologists, hollowed-out bi-planes, trepanned obscura, verboten chairs, sand split camera sculls, sifting coursed mineral, funeral rain stains virescent steps, calcified Franks walk beside lace flyovers, hands sodden, gripping eyelash fences, reading matter bleeding fluorescent black bile, troughs of cerulean honey channel conciliatory vomit into this criss-cross garden, hitching untrustworthy pieces of insight into a sweetened rust bowl, greased and ready to hang sects, unsightly rhapsodies of lead statues breed, listen for lapping instructions, pitching unpalatable taxonomies, under-tooled stay standing, grow well amongst under-cultivated Goths, slightly pustulated, untroubled by parts of a day, over extended, unindented sounds, eventually covered moss, untitle all snaps, a sore of epochs, explanatory films on mitochondrial screams, whatever glue unlocks, matter understands sub-matter, esteemed blisters, glass replacing grass, wind blown faces standing for leaden windows, bricked up choir drains, disinvestment choral stains, still snow falls like soot, tooth-scrapped fissures, rot trimmed voices, plaque teeming, perceive meaning perceived, newly fotoed, look intended, hanging from shaved walls, conclude reproduction, quietly stand at gate yellow, what marks made of unusual behaviour, remember unnoticed endeavours, untrimmed friends gnaw through remaining cells, thin excretus laid over crusts, mistimed noises, sound-like salt, retorts amplify unsociable contradictions, unreasonable antipathies, chairs of scribbled grist, floors of sore weave, hideaways list unattended classrooms, voices pour rattle coins from a sack, cities invoke night falls, weeping radio pocks, starved heat, walls under furniture, enemy alabaster, razor flavour ice-cream, whose death replays clock sticking chatter, callused-back mirror, armed clatter, faint looks shade these tepid days, sunny fall, causeway swept, road jars, positioning glass, house plates prevent sensitised holes, amber bloom of unfixed silver-salts, excuse without excuse, live through any time we can, being unaligned, menace parabolas, indicate curving, cuckold bend, seaside telemetry, isometric undertaker, tag synaesthesia, directions contradict, wash time, widen wires, hear a hiss of cracking plates, thumb bleed, claim calm afternoons, ectomorphs replacing trees in Versailles, forest stories bifurcate, road-weary lacemakers soled our unseasonal shoes, walked forbidden corridors, pocket basted stones, cynical guts, iconoclasts' scarfs, Rue du Temple agreement, removes job-burning books, she looks at silences, lucid maintenance, cope occasions, defence synonymies, out-louding sea, unsure return cranium, shores always leak ships, leave shelters for shelters, invitation wound, tightly inverse, sleeping on hats, beside moors, moiré fizzing, sheltering behind froth, keeping spray, repeat waking, mailed none things, high walled groove, relentless tepidness, rain empty rooms, distrait quietus, disproportional conjecture, liquid faces, incessant splatter, indivisible plane, immaterial contrast, transparent whine, fear disapproval, bodging lathes, chair machines, electrode skin, tongue the walls, become narrative, m-brane suck, fly-blown integument, divided sounds, bi-line drizzle, discordant antonyms, miscarried voices, kinetic solitude, disoriented light, dusty bats, medium information, informationless for art, setting stales, moment attentiveness, hard locked doors, squealing realise, finders' door, key for all, fear indented, alabaster key, fortunate inquisitor, instrumental views, call locking, stick greens to calm unshaved iron.

Unnamed month, spoke only, inexpressible appropriate, year alarum, unlit rendering, actions suspect, word ground, given restrict, room necessity, attend tedium, troubling yield, olid savagery, contagion rather, endure obloquy, venturing doors, choosing whispering, street lonely, moved apologetically, eye expectation, social never, middle interchange, gutter entertain, however moment, around existential, lacuna populous, ineluctably impelled, gather seeping, together houses, pavement armada, shame grinding, through square, where wood, converge central, churning speechless, miasmatic antipathy.

Centre squared presentiment, language sticks, mound clamber, gathering bustle, turn puzzle, awe gesticulate, recite tone, formed etherial, utterance imitation, born transfixion, murmurs ease, ripple gathering, button coinage, jewelled cobbles, ripped cheep, ground showered, upon unfortunate, broken rapture and mass tragic, incantation rupture, sayer drained, bewildered through channels, entrancing drain holes of home.

Thousands Degree Shade

Knocked over footsteps, a listening breath on crumbling wood, no open reply, in whisper, there is ease, until imagined slow standing, at border parts, journeys carve heavy, on this gaseous island, type is complete on body paperwork, sign in for a do not way, sistered absolution, drying snow flakes on leafy tongue, spell illegible once supped enough, wrote head glasses hang from a crumbling neck, from rung morning, peaceful nights amongst thousand degree shadows. Cry for neonate, which grow to crumble, losing flowers like jellied haystacks, or running ells, tripping hats to headless ornaments, in the leadened stream, sculpted gargoyles mix pointing wine with verdigris rain, filtering birds through dissolving gutters and canticles through diseased pipes. Too cold now to collect unwalled suitcases. Granddad made it home, his room intact under his bed, vast closed planes are needed, interchangeable years before the war, apt Village fashions adapt, only to fall from high steps of an industrial Italian tower.

Lineless

Boarderless which being intent denies, pursued by trails of ash stained snow, through emptier woods swarming with calls, unstable atavists crawling on crumbling mounds of insubstantial walls, crimes against insanity proclaimed across this indeterminate Village. Wandering irresolute streets, watching many forms of sweat drip, brume drifts about brittle lanes, immersing throttled houses, and mosaic stones crack slightly by design, infant cobbles creak, violently settling underfoot in drizzle rhyme, trickling from mouths of each abject object, square lined slaver of craven picaroon greedily cawing this sticky ground, between slabs of melting flesh-like bleeds, sore bronze and charred welts adorning stone angels, attest to wanton carnality, cruel impassiveness, tricking grimaces lost in reflection, grown tired windows of each cottage, with weathered belts they tethered themselves, cracked grey skin gnawed a little, numb girdling hands ground more foulness into weeping pores, beneath streets of muffled whimpers, around dreaming creatures, filtered through crannies of Village voices, overheard inhabitants peck and crow, childbed to dirt-bed, deafening of visitors, barely resonant directions, emotion-like absence, tepid paper events, Village complete by running as a fissure, dispirited as a disparate, upturned tale as untuned contrivance, unbridged homogeny, a mass mottle of unblemished entities, distinguishing drift of over-settled snowflakes, or corralled rake-bites, moments trickled as a bourn through shifting seams, Village witnessing light felled from things, dissolve reforming resolve, surface ladder to telescopic pattern, chronic aberration of chromatic reflection, concave extremis, scorched thoughts are calm apparent, blistered flaking into translucency.

A studded grind, saddened by a miss-call, relayed echo amid distant sleep, recumbent crowded seeping rooms, a listening night shout into the congested spirals of grass burnt hills, morning Village smoke valley waved, light day secreting fragrant veiling, where discernible word gestures distort, and insoluble activities evoke unaccountable images of unsought tales told through a wall.

INgrain

A view of an ingrained mirror, source encoded by unfathomed anteons, activate unresolved dithering, where oiled ashen untraceable glances race in intractable steps, and pale tenebrous c-types take token immolation for tepid imitation, though tunnel-ticking lights, eye-scratching mesmerism, road rhythms call quietly beyond a window, caressing wakes, misshapen states crossing subtropical paths, chatting tides outside graze dismembered arsenic lights, holding to behind atomic mouth-pieces, interflowing monochrome pasts inevitably form, there in a wood where nobody stood, restives diminish in their lime-light.

Stairs of a hundredth storey, at a window on an escaping city, odious suns mist acrid red, sour night air crawls and claws the glass, speaking quietly from the bed, through many pallid days and overexposed nights, craving to wait at the window, anew to listen, in an undefined morning, as warring rocks wear to sand.

Unlit substances leach distorted feculent glass, unchanging smears which avoid unruly gaze, grubbing through sordid silica, stand pleading passing revenants, for worlds made different.

We are the hungry ones, we are the unbelieved ones, we sit beneath headless towers swaying and crumbling from disregarded words which howl into these callous walls.

Acidulous rain burns through the thinning hat of a man with no voice, others gather beside a caliginous drawing of a fractal building, hidden by daylight, empyrean wasteland beckons neatly fouled hearts, coarse septimes' unease suggested draining distance behind this mirror immaterial, roads absorb gilded skis, travellers dismisses horizons, ways trample their own ground, track made naked feet lead towards a silhouetted howe, unassailable walls trail green sticks in molten waters, as flakelets burn into the back of a solitary pourer.

Beached footprints leach onto rusting beds, the musty room flakes in this beside-the-sea-salt hotel, damp grey edgeless days sallow, amorphous hours enter this uncluttered room, unfolded suitcase, packed with shame and regret, words catch in the lamp light, distance drizzled against low skies, a weeping sea levigated stirring rocks, grinding a fetid aerosphere, rivers fret through unnamed towns, hundred-thousand flies drown in vented gutters and gold-leafed sewers, a feebly puling sea embrocates waxen steps, polished handrails barbed with ink stained pen nibs, with tightly grasping hands, ink-blood spiralled this involuted iron-webbed staircase, far down to a long forgotten banquet.

A habituated husk of presumptive waste, accepted helplessness beneath an unstopped clocktower, on Place Quatre Porte, grubby rain bridge gathers, drenching evening suicides, who scratch face paint from the bridgehead saint guarding the rot of an unsinkable rêve, là où est le fleuve, lamp-posts scatter, ordered deceit, flurried regimen, where horizons steep and all reflections are vile.

Cracked open outdoor rooms of impenetrable expression, words fired at opposing walls broke Anning reliquiae which upturned bled into damp stones, desaturating those intolerable voices of an insoluble room. Old at a touch, sit on this end pillar of a last wall before the remaining unlit road, sounds of future rings are stifled, only etiolate visions now form as shadowless planes on which to rest, seeded desires now wither and on which path, drawn from pockets of rock to stone to gravel, to take to clear this Village is unchoiced.

Ausländer

Silence folds a flow of cries, tributary gash on unlaced hands pulls apart a neatly bifurcated haemorrhage, separating rotten grains within the hem of a septic core, self selecting on-lookers contrive to watch shallow splinters being pulled from within suppurating out-houses, bilingual bowmen obviate the drip of blackened carcasses across Northern French fields, cutting through oblate vowels and seams of freshly crafted ravines suits this wild assemblage, an imperative ingress to batter this old city, disassembling all traditional inclinations bridge birds calmly peel heads from horse-hair ells, transparent gatekeepers affect to lock out occasional onlookers, at Aragon Point passers pallor at friendly fire, puling at dry tides, citing Grieg while ditching blocks which felled bourgeoise waltzing over a tailor-made crossing, jam for mortar, this floor is a non-floor floor consecrated for kissing unenshroudable cousins, unburdened by nailed-to bricks brought to decorate high walls of drifting kite-ward towers, gentle heads can again rest amid spikes and wait beside the last runny spot of greenery, gracing all unploughed concrete with a blemish, criss-crossing cured skin, before returning to belligerent quietude, rising unseasonably to stand calmer in fields of fretted white, waking softly toward unprinted images of dusk, too proud to pillory an unanchored stock, being here, knowing here, degaussing a hostile lock, a gut long spoon purchased with intention to hammer out sordid lines, as haughty scholars with solar stiffened collars discover in their hollow hands the weight of discontinued aspiration, this tedium of legless chairs and ingratitude of those tender lives they are enjoined to cell-cowled embellishingly abridge.

The End of Suicide

Calluses about each arm trace lines of a blackening seascape, on wasting rock she touches the tips of each hair, this scalding keel hails an adamantine vessel boiling windblown winter canvas, stepping back foot aground, time-bound travellers who misspelled land, slipped their scrips between splintered decks, a prick of blood between knotted ropes of cloth pulls back the rock, asserting cause shall uncloak the machine, to wake as an unspinning wheel, entering spiralling lifts which ascend on shaky wires, a feckless innocent tiptoes before a lean audience, looks incredulous out across empty velvety seats and over web-like crumbling matter of a slime-lit arch, while in the wings pulling at the hanging strings which make fast the hands of the side- eyed audience, puppeting a collective clap-clap at the peddling act, the automaton sceptical at reaching the sticky isles, in pointed innuendo, ran gracelessly between grimacing crowds, through unhinged doors to a version of outside, just as blue fires crackle far along the streets of straw, bringing down a sinew of hostels, until enshrouding this Pocket-Book Theatre in divers scented smoke. The end of suicide. Footnoted, infant Fortunate chewed on an intendant daughter's furless marionette, mouth stuffed and unwashed, she shuffled beneath each bed, a quick round of sniffed feet, before curling up to sleep below these many ceilings of dripping whitewash. Instantly, though not inside the furtive cavity, this leaden leader looked down at the masticated boots of each ragged tinner, who dusting off what they took to be camouflage, nipped at a whale-bone basket's bending L through rotting frames while hooking the ram-sacks from spherical urns, then raising the retching lids on these bandy-thighed bandits, agreed to be borne and displayed alongside those puddles of barbarous faux hair, seized pacemakers, a collection of insensitive whispers, and a trawled box of miscellaneous used tissues. Yet hope tinkles over all, and on occasion forms a semblance of possible discontent. Behind this collective apparition is the shape of an empty chair, here amid inaudible calls, a half-turned figure chants an unmemorable incantation read from an old postcard, a relic chanced upon somewhere by someone, perhaps down the back of a disinherited Ford Zephyr seat, engirdled by beacon wavers who turn on the lustful, the unhinged and disinclines sweeping in confused alarm over an enervated fetaloge, and out along a fetid channel towards a whistling, no, whining drain. Now, the purpose of the greedy is to prise the preset from the general scattering of unabashed impotents, disembodied pigmentaries, and elephantine prenuptial parents. Ah, vociferates the neighbour from behind an unplanned obstacle, gobs of grubby sweat rivulating unsociable patterns between folds and undulatory pensile fat, in dead stare theorising, be it a casket or a basket, imperatives first, bent nails must be sewn through each corner to bind the untidy straw, tease arachnids out through the draughty gap, wave at those passing under the pavement, dirty the skirting with lemon, ground teasel and mutton-cherries, pass the superannuated crate over the seeping wall to the cackling old bat who waits, nets dripping and rivet-grinned, on the corner of Canning Road for a fine delousing. Reaching the overlooked canal, dusted by an ossified Ponte dei Sospiri, at an unblemished hour, disregarding the bobbing Capuchin sculls and their pickled-in-oil refractory beards, follow the coercing of a long trousered oversensitive inundate, who once bedded down for a time between the de-pointed brickwork of a desanctified alehouse and a woman who daily beat the walls of a minor shit-house with a sickly stick and, upon a many moon-scratched night, scrawled an elegant tractate on the ideals of mock onto the inside of her hat and nailed it to his head, before wandering off towards Glasscoat Road, where she was last seen crawling under the whinnying door of the arcade's remaining thirdhand emporium.

So it begins, scheme one a, ice over the shutter, wedge open the squealing sycamore doors and feign to cower before the insouciant and atypical Latin paintings, which, no longer in a box, become simply a collection of fomenting, de-agonised images, instruments no more wondrous than that of an under-flannelled butcher's slab. Grazing promptly onto b, retaliation, peg out eight premonitory corners, taking the yew as primary altar, and a large ferret-lined bag in which to hide the necessary delft, sidle toward the ineffable chair and pilfer from beneath the temporary stand vulcanised drippings from the melting letters of The Intacita Proclamation, hide these in an uninterrogated fold. And on and on and so, up to numeral y, where unprepossessing but disquieting, a campanologist wrestles with a tip-toe tie-rope, occasioning spiral flutterings of dislodged suitors, invigorating and occasioning a collective belief that spectacle will solicit an ebullient masquerade of pyroclastic exuberance, and from this usual pallid, a queasy and unnecessary gathering is instigated. Yet, in extremis, as flags crack, the path overgrows with parchment, and fragments of unheard speeches confetti down to the orifices of gawping, grime- straddled masses, on the edge of the scene a cleft stick wilts against a tree, flapping exigent envelopes, irritating its fork, as greasy sheets cover inevitably flaking traces of inappropriate ink, marks of dried spittle and withering white finger stains, all of which seem to substantiate the veracity of the folk tale of Concave Mountain, a story, in brief, of how the communal outpourings of accumulated bile of an unaccountable dyspeptic Village uprooted then evanesced a not insubstantial mountain, which it is claimed, was unfortunate, not to say ironic, as the Concave Mountain had always proved to be a reliable if not inexhaustible source of a bitter brown alkaline universally known as Ciis, an impotent yet seductively diverting elixir. Hmm. Concerning the digression, M. D., it is indeed possible to follow activities favoured by those beau monde of the vitiated Village, with tangential methodologies, such as memorising names ripped from backs of mirrors of unpalatable likenesses, placing dark-clothed alchemists in a crock, allowed to breed into a vague puddle of letters, stimulating a release of spores, finally reforming these odd and ever mutable cells into a simple yet elegant landscape likeness of Eilean Ghruinneard. The hysterical few would perhaps wish to attend to their responsibilities and huddle under an empty shell, and while pointing to the shouting figure, reflect upon the last corner of glass in the sole window of the not too far away tower. The minions, meanwhile, might stand face in hands, sobbing to summer murk filtering through screaming trees, their woe parodying profuse and ponderous retorts to Mr. Turmzeit's timorous declarations, scribbling lines of life on a stick, and aspiring a future for all ill-defined landscapes, to be assayed and qualified as no smaller than a customary listening vent and no larger than the length of an horizon one can amble in a day. But yet on all arms burn-lines stink, festering further in the gelatine air of this unsavoury valley, where to consider stepping towards meandering rills is to exercise absurd yet clearly common expectation that the unseemingly vast vista seen from any point in the Village, does remain concealed by a mass of overwrought green spikes stapled on to the caliginous hillside, over which an array of epigrams dazzle the viewer into believing the course of the conceited river, which winds between so many comely and disturbing meadows, does indeed flow on to an imaginary untraversable sea, where countless blooded horizons boil, and windblown skies dab and swaddle unsealable wounds.

Unrest

The Village stands cold before a remote sun. Time has wept from these tapping streets, stone walls now ring as unkeen cracked shells, beside undyed front doors, uncertain winds quietly peal hooks of many small bells, clematis' screams echo out as it climbs and constricts perishing wooden weave, small mounds amongst the houses guide streams to calloused leaden sewers, ancient mossy steps up to infant high doors chafe at indweller's foot wear, windows' grime-dried faces deaden reflections, graining invisible any substance beyond their insoluble barricade. From sundown, translucent figures push through the gossamer quiet street lights, the susurration of going home across cobble skulls for craven suppers and altogether drink stanchions the insinuated call of unrest.

Silent Street

Outside children sing, what shall we be today, count twenty arbitrary words, and hand by hand circled. No meaning, no information. Where is there to write on days like these,
q e b d

beneath the many wasting rocks, where a tree falls in the desert no one hears it howl, where through an open box we breathe, let the train run on to one more station, just the other side of the border, where rows amid rows of silent chairs wait for us to stumble, while wasting and warring over upended words, a wreathed eye weathered to an uneasy hymn, no exit clues in the margins, like footprints in silicone dust, waking to the sense of falling grains which pepper faces backing away from the calm, resigned to intramural migrations, gentle old hands hiding the sores settle down the dry bedrock from which our berth is worn and pillars are formed by many an antipathetic kiss.

For the worth of all words came to nothing, any mote of meaning there might have been of the smallest gesture was no longer sought for, and the lights in the distance shone, cold and indifferent, no longer watched, as they were found to be no longer distant. And the world ended on Silent Street.

Rattle's Alley

Unmoving as a film razored still, in that radio voice which ghosts about oxidising stairwells, the dim light through which it reverberated made sponges of the granular air, one avenue along which to explore was a corridor leading to a door which swung open to the translucent cry of an apparent figure standing wrapped in a crepuscular field. Words were not words perched fishing from the mantlepiece, a paper fantasy writing itself along blank lines, sitting a while reflecting on its own image, as sounds crawling from the fabric began scratching at the floor, peeling cognates from context, snapping at divergences, jointed vacancies, with incubated whispers, lines tore from lines, peppering bitterness onto orotund lips, forming cerulean letters for the blistering and underdressed firmament. Days were lost amongst the myriad sunwashed streets of this ancient Village, finding etherial visions projected against the blistering lofty houses of a midnight Arcadian square, they fell to watching a salt line of attentive visitors gather along damp banks, tapping the water with long ripe willow, the bones at their feet hidden amongst potholed power lines, strings measuring strings so collapsing the wave form, those being unversed in Newtonian barking and gauging the incertitude of a packet of high scent bergs, yet beyond the membrane fence we dress as the neighbours dress, eating into disregarded niceties with ferocious distain, rogue eggs bleating, swans dribbling foul ululations into the greasy wine, the faces turn and knees crease, tall children cease teasing ineffectual parents, and beyond the line across the harlequin lawn a volley of glass beads pelted the heads of the tormented, a well meaning convocation of damp indulgents who ignored Pheidippides scattered in stabbed abandon across the expanse of mud, less equipped bodies hide behind the mounds of well combed Trojan hair, further into the damp land, behind the upturned parsonical hovel, a scattering of neophytes, refusing to attend to their new sayer and the unpalatable disillusions, sits within the ring of gathering scioptic ball makers, who scowl at their view of overturned patents, likewise, farriers' excursions into intercontinental balloon production gave ascendancy to sighing Burghers, malodorous doctors dishing calisthenic pills to disperse impatient audiences, unaccountable mothers and immaterial shoppers wait and wait, while scouts giggle behind piles of prehistoric wicker pots, street cleaners quietly de-interlace the word forms engraved into the creasing rafters, and sootcasters harvest swarf from the floors about the feet of urinating matchmakers gathered outside the Eschian walled garden, oblivious to the swathes of migrating savants picking sea shells from the dying sea shore. Some aeons passed, and in the teeming dark houses dripping glass began to fissure, and sanguine bodies, streaming head down into the low lit avenues, coursed towards the unmoved river and, blithely stepping in, each saline form whimpered and dissolved. In the overlooking, unsupported tower, many layers of moist words, serving as a bouncy floor, began drying, before fracturing underfoot, liberating their bitter causticity, and rendering the hyperventilating painter, pronounced a demigod by the screaming clergy, exhausted, and so exhorted by his stair-mass muses to place an ear to his intolerable work, and listen for the hollow-drawn figures walking to his door, relent and sit facing the wall as they exculpate or endow him for his fine work as just another unnecessary marketeer. The years squandered, and with no subject on which to lie, nor appetite on which to ponder, through curtained alleys, the imaginator arrived at the corridor and at length this balcony, the half implied muffled chair was, as delineated by the illuminated contract, posited towards the end of the gangplank. Easing into the musty fabric and creaking frame, the professional dreamer sat comfortably, looking down, watching as the noisome, toiling throng stacked miscellaneous furniture in the centre of that great, drippingly illuminate chamber, where all six mirror-lined walls were cracked, a horde of tearful candles wept at the scene, and calcified beasts teetered on high stone pilaster continued to fade. Out beyond the seven encrusted doors, the old bleeding hands of hand-passing rows pressed on, heaping splintered objects upon splintering objects, counting each to each in horse voices, as starved forebears logged forms in well scripted lines of putrid ink on perishing parchment, huddling for warmth beside the fuggy fat lamps. Up at the great glass and iron canopy, the writer remembers to wake and watch the world as it fights on without him.

Sentinel

Voices writhe on keen spikes drawn high above moon ground roads carrion pick dripping words where evening currents play inoffensive babble at sonicated legislators communicating in mini blurs between corners of fly vile ground and unfenced marches resting heavily at crumbs quarter amongst pecks and siren fading talons retching against an unguarded bridgehead wash ebbing as ancillary cranes darken against impasto sundowns for it was once slurred tedium is the illness of waking up to a snake full of moths who call while wet recalling overheard passing planes and gossip of fornicating sonorists where junior romantics chatter to nightly brothers on a pale couch of red-headed stepchildren and villagers resolve to pass above mountains of shells stinking before the gates gathered to stain the restored Celtic edifice where signs of under-turns are reflections on barbarisms waiting on a long bench alongside disunioned vernacular mounds recalling wreckage written down twice before the tall field waterside as piles of boats spread out over rough grit grazed ground for gloved hand images of alabaster glasses and stone ring tones to release somnambular pictures of enticing letter splintering cavalries to give way at the weigh-station their calls carrying reports of weather to seeded oolitic hearts before tailing animate writing written in the wrong chair the air is on its way should lighter colours suggest anomalous fortifications as tin bronze eyelids are cast in the finest mud in preparation for seduction.

Pleasantly Imbalanced

Pleasantly imbalanced on croaking shields neutered councillors embrace the combined insubstantial guests' breaths, the prize is the wait, on naked ice the expectants gather, mucilage is served into cupped hands, ground is given to a stampede of breakaway prognosticators, whose graven teeth glance down onto an indecorous throng looking up from the incandescent footings of this inverted wooden henge, where legless chairs are stored and putative enthusiasts for dismantling banquets vie for footprints stuck to a wall, indivisible sacks of Neolithic clothing are sonorously unidentifiable, the unseasonably vibrant b-listers caress the outside of the iron-strap clad chests, as demi-cooked relatives stand once more waiting to be read at, immobile ploughs cast from de-hinged nail clad doors are illuminated in crusty paint, a suggested bomb impedes the flow of a waterborne pollution of lacquer, and as disconsolate plaster saints trail behind, small notes are disseminated amongst the dispersing populace, who are lately found beside the lachrymose lake, milling about a disrobed ersatz dissembler kneeling before the insubstantial bastion, who from the straplog pier watches a sardonic paean slowly flake and drift over the disillusioned immaterial mass.

Over Western Docks

Through Western Docks we crawl, fume framed exemplars swinging eschew, farrier bound feet dance and no one in the crowd dampens the pitch. Aligned benches drip-dry in this empty Autumn park, crawling home, the discomposed pulled in fear by matter dreary skies, in a frayed pocket fear-scarred pictures show soldiers enjoined to carry glass-bottomed silver, through high damp windows, under nihilist papers wired authors sit in hanged heat prising open lives of a damp generation, from a blistering ceiling wet acid-yellow leaves flit hopelessly resigned to a worn woven floor, another day observing is something to be observed. Now feathered antecedents walk waning yellow lines to the end of a street where a great hole fumes, here gather many clacking comments in pestilential voices, waiting with backs to the edge no one pushes or pockets the cakes falling to the street, beyond the rails books are placed as cats-eyes along the flyover, the binding of the genteel invaders' thumbs itch a little, deleted November suns often shone, as now, burning a wake across fallen white fields into the rootful forest, on this dissolving day nose-haired elites walk the needlepoint paths, charcoal trees drawing allegories on their undisguised bodies, on the floor amid mottled thistledown armed flocks of desquamate uproot to the cliff faces, while a new generation of irritable bystanders continue to claw at the ice, up above, walking inset margins, taping those who over smile, underrepresented water-trappers dependent on frosty wires speak in elegiac pitch to the great hanging ceiling, in the smaller halls, hobble- and tap-webbed familiars caress the napes of ignorant Jerumites, and flatland families rattle overbearing concrete supports, at the more imprecise extremities, a remaining few Cimmerians forgot to screw the fan back into the crest above

the neat nest built into the noise of the old mechanism, and
beyond the isle, as the seas sank, the last ships pulled to a halt
against a drawing of an old iron pier.

Night Train from Liège

I look out across the ornament of Nürnberg, between shadows of speechless streets and dark eyed buildings, yellow greased faces and grieving dry sweat, facades waited pent beneath dripping hollow lights. Awake at 4.20 am, where the view from the carriage window is a composition of lights across a hill. As the train approaches Passau, I see clearly my home town.

Shutting Down

Impurities gather to form soiled state perturbations, despised communicators worm towards other atavistic embellishments, a blemish of elementals mutate forming borders and annihilating language, lengthening hours seep through paper, a chain strung between thin blooded fauna and strapless trees' expeditious branches pull tighter, pushing dough into antipodean ruptures and fuel between finely etched teeth, weather coloured hair bonds between brides, assailing their knotted sap in a wreckage of disassociation, bleeding from occidental fabric fuse wire knits itself into the margins. Land now and walk amongst a caw of sitting figures picking at the roots with darting tongues, at some distance irregular clouds coalesce, small stones break into a sweat, pull back, and the scene is set for this Village of noble reptiles, lazing amongst the far away noise of bleating nomads, slide beneath the glass for trinocular inspection, beating back a rush of foresights imitating grimy gestures, see teeth grate on crumbs, tongues tastefully while away, heavy eyes unblinkered rest beside the gates, at grieving posts the overformed stay as mute as hungry dancers turning the iron floor to stinking mud, waiting below gun towers lost envelopes remain unsealed, timid officers gleefully adrift peel caulkin from blown-over skiffs, old cork tirelessly disentangling the string of words crawling from the castle windows, pitted walls bathe in the shimmering miasmatic moat, as an immune Suram began once more mapping out a new fortress.

Iota

Junctions between Munich's level grounds and innocent substrata recoil at the workers' rotting breath. Jettisoned screams flake down to a burning road, where mountainous flesh races about conical beds scattering fledgling figurines. Janus keeps trip rooms at the weigh station, calling on granular car park surveyors to escape unless sub-scribed. Juno creeps towards a vein of far leaves, cramming into the well nothing to explain its colour collapse. July kicks wrecked drips over hilled spurs, creasing these felled fallow indents. Jasmin engages rage amongst twin strangers, on which tall column its failed labourers unsignalled lent, validating the insignificant bascule of polluting lamps fleeting from the depths Königsplatz sighs.

Marianne Moore is the Girl with the Pearl Earring

Let us travel by compass, with a heading set towards the face of startling fields, not following but leaving behind us a path of trodden damp grass, as a lens based painting is how we thought we thought, with distemper dripping hair, we never met, beside your ringing necks, if they turn and twist, tenderly unloved, enticing future hands, pictures of fragile dimension, calling forever, there is another besides who has worn that look.

Edges

It has gone now, the walk to the canal, the trail lost leading to this water's edge, broken stones, here under a waked storm, sullen breaths scratching like teeth at web-worn windows, where small houses could be no blacker, streets whiter, harsh blocks of stygian ink just holding from bleeding into the pallid paper, we waited where the road ended and the unbounded planes began, the towers far behind us, the Village knotted at the gnarled feet of the pellucid mountains before us.

Insanitary Bite

A shower of grit cracks the walls where the sea does not count sway. In a time beside the prostrate sea, a perfect wave haled over the beach to those waxen feet as they stood in line waiting for the steam to lift and reveal the insurgent tides, as quiet as voices gambolled in easy breath along the shore, on this, another amber morning. Writing of time, this inability to work against elemental desires is fathomable, it is as a prelude to waking though the abstracted night, to flee far from evasive visions, crying at the beauty of the concrete pillars before dismantling them with callous fingers and incendiary bites. Stepping from these cushions at the river's edge, far downstream, just before where water evaporates, they follow a corrupted air, as it plunges through the soft mask of leaden sails, savouring those peeling crusts of previous vistas, the corrosiveness of forgetfulness eats deep into an unsuccessful mind. Enter the fadelands of the unvisited parts of the city, places which only exist where arcades, unpeopled streets and interlinking tunnels are backed into, there are no agoraphobics in this crumbling marketplace, no open carriages from which to observe abandoned streets, no unboarded glass on which to breathe, and from which to follow the reflection of a myriad lights as they flare dully across the wet city, and a sinking sun makes shadows of its tribes. Soundless drumming faces, desperate for the unuttered weeping of an unoccupied world, that noiseless stare through which each fugacious form remains visible.

If I Wake Then What Shall I Do

What sum are we
Lapsed apprehensives
    a coagulate of failings
    a mirth of dreams
    ripping wishes from disillusion
Nothing silent ever enters by a door
Slicing into another morning of irrationality
A tear in the scenery
Carnivorous lenses
A page of text over which to write
From here in the wood where the undecided stood
My dreams are webs your hands spiders
What a world we might have made.

Waive

Occasionally you break into an honest voice, she said, her head sitting amongst the stilled ships, a play of air convulsing through those misshapen cracks between uncorked beams, her sensitive reflections misunderstanding recollections. I am yet to find my substitute, she writes, and what do I know other than those I imagine. Approaching a fantasy renders it impotent, so says the night. She whispers to the blank page, a great work of art was never newly made, it has always existed. Wait one more minute, one more stroke of a hand, here, beside the lamp, do not touch your face, as impatient fear, look, I will hold up my watch, you will see how quickly this day will pass. Silently she writes through the night, ink-less fingers miming copious accounts across this empty table, this island, this frame around a longing house, delivered by boat, the visitor outside, her aged face gone with the blowing off of her hat, speaks only to me, and the ancient gods behind the ruin's door prey on my quietly howling hours.

Fourth Night

This night stop train this stream to stop draining rotting thoughts stop your slowing steps where you pull us through this fourth fifth morning which cannot stop having what lies beneath you stop these same routines stop ways and bending from a saline ground calls stop through this broken lock indulgences stop this is not a way to fail to stop go through these rounding trees and untenable rasping air where feeling fails stop reopening the weary game' forty-nine forty-nine forty-nine I must eat these words around me too stop counting then continue in tiresome grasping imagination stop this majestical roof and amongst the rolling hills animated by light I stop again I stop and am on the fortieth step stop the date it is the four-hundredth day of the four-thousandth month and the last stop and across a snowdrift sky I stop staring out.

For Méliès

I continue to write in the mist, words describing what I see through the seeping words I write on the steamed glass. Méliès dreams have become a comb. The underlying graphic of worn architecture is now an insensible structure, a torn manifesto, written during the early age of the photographic image. Here everyone is angry, each tasting their last embers and evermore bafflement. From your fifth floor chair you contemplate the vast crowd facing away from you, infrequently rising to step to your window, where below, in fading light, you regard the tearful figure who stands alone on the great concrete plane, looking up, searching the still windows for you.

Parasite Paradise

As time leaks from each face, burning air washes the feet of the crowd, murmurs of a memory pass amongst the mass, low roofed children stare down, their hair plucked by rare birds who nest unseen amongst ringing walls, and these engrafted houses, suck within a stockpile of depleting lives, decaying in their own time.

Roadside

Restlessness drowns in slow tides, in a burden of eloquence, a wreckage of sunsets, a simmering road of tangling ropes tether those whitewashed voices warped by sedimentary postholes, where crawling words caw alone on plates, speechlessness shackled by appeals to indistinct close-ups, implicated in itinerant code, worming around adzed ashes, a line of delicate scrawls in dampening sand marks each grain for successors to find, waiting on a roadside reading the veins of particulates, passing chewing fat down the ancestral line, road-kill gods being foregone delusions, trams grasp at steaming streets, tramps parody life at home, caressed by torrential sameness and grave inserts, bottled callus' all fail to birth, twisted vitals eaten at the a.m., blown beside by all the giddy meek, the fell of yesterday spear the coming dilation of unleadend breasts, breath on paper, words on spit, short runs and all back to the screaming room where x and y axes wait to enthral, an acre of tethered giggles land-locks curlicues hardwired into curdling whispers, plucking at the picket screens, televisionaries place metropols on the set of the crime, they who leer at the couch, tucking into wet guardians, encouraging the forty or so blades to sit up, handing out dance cards, unfettered by paper coins, unmaskable faces pooling in the heat of the Bauhaus walls, germs crawling from a pocket watch, perfume dries on the pewter plate, and the exposed key is a weight about the children's corrosive corrective, canned grass is on picnic watch, the hidden unlocks the visible, reviving unfocused calpate nights, palpate over-mouthed oikophobics, lies agree with the maker of the open drawer, where a burden of fabricators sleep secure in their own shit, favoured by the pirouettes who decorate their unlocked wounds, they shout down every resolve, mimicking the rolling grimaces of the uncoloured ones, who daily cry of grief, four to a basket, ringing a paper bell, and call across the land in a long abandoned stare.

Distant Absence

Thoughts gathered at the tip of the pen, a bright chimera called day, walking branching paths, passing rill-barked trees blossoming amongst incensed walls of long forgotten homes, which when walked towards fall further into absence, taking a holiday on street view, intolerable as an air flight, unsavoury as a flea bite, bastardised chronology, overscreened morphology, undead information, slaughter approbation, only unintelligence makes art, unfolding himself, he began telling of a woman who, threadbare amongst towering ruins, wandered amongst smoky cellars and rank tunnels beneath a dehydrating sea, and in one foggy land the people never blinked, in another the people never opened their eyes.

Dilation

There was symmetry between incalibrate voices shouting into the octus crowd from behind damp curtains, as along the gleaming hollow way everyone hides, where once was shadow sun-light now flooded the turbid streets, protectors fell from a cot, in a house with snakes for stair rods and razors for stairs, the oriflamme kettle on, weeping alongside antiseptic visitors, tall like many hallucinating mannequins eating into the vocalist's a-side, astride the boiling fire burning beneath the mantle, an ornate thespian orates a tale of five-and-twenty unhappy chapmen lolling from the symposium towards home, telling stories of lost apathy and how keen their letters to the Siliconians are, meaning, she said, is like the force of gravity, insubstantial and gruelling when too much time is spent in it, a word when fascicled with many others can burn through a hand, the dying flesh forming pale grey images before flaking onto single tracks or into the cracks of an empty car park, alongside mind-lice which fall from the mouths of wanderers who have yet to tire, in this and every world without margins, every happy moment ends in doleful memory.

Dark Under Sunrise

Coarse thirteens fade nailed wearing stole sole stale stained overcoat, blackened mount seeps steps steeps unevenly greasy porch, glancing lights beneath door heavy fibrous, game taping trapping tripping window frames block glass out outside, picture grass taste trace traipse last coloured snow, shallow torpid pedestrian gains grains grants marrow evince, leaking whispers caught wall wail waste words, effervescent particulates, ineffable inaccessible incompatible taste continuous unsustainable unattainable unsellable.

Tyranny

Illness froths onto the sloping table, above the overweight Hanoverian box an over tortured mirror etches on the glass someone else, the ha'penny-press reports there are dead flies in the undertaker's window again, cloud painting media make a ballet of the inconsequential, begin another day tomorrow, Borough gains does love incidental landscapes, overgleened self-portraits are waste beside this undertrusted road, pledged states embrace the post-interesting and inept illusionaries, longanimity, like music in an empty house or Degas' At the Cafe, shouts through the scarcely adjacent window astonishing the disapproving incipients, coronal put-upon day, to the town the red wash is delivered, rolling alongside the recoiling canon the hammocked bowmen tire of the formulated info-ads featuring equatorial fletchers, gangrene appetisers silvered before unarmoured epiphytes who audience the unfaithful Broom line duel with the waterborne Bear-shirts, unflossed putti standing by with tarpaulin and hemp to carry off ever unappealing coronates, from a cold hill the attending Dagon-hatter plastic bagging the regulation hypothecate, a katabatic event adding more fluff to the bedside jar.

Paper Day

She stopped me in the street and asked if we own what we see. She told me she had read Tolstoy and wanted to live by the sea, where her memories could come in waves and the distant views had not changed for a dozen lifetimes. I waited for her to return to me, writing to her every day about how the cities' facades were peeling away from their past, and how nobody looked at the floor anymore, but only through the faces of passers by. Her letters were long and evasive, full of need and gentle frustrations, as though she were haunting the world, unable to touch anything, save reflections and shadows. We walked through our pages together as though through our own unfathomable streets, putting on each other's skin, looking to experience the way the other does. Until the day the letters sent were empty, the folds were composed and the many leaves full, but there were no more shadows cast across the page.

Blank

Crawling beneath sunlit fog, sharing cooler air, a shaded creature absorbs deliquescent fibres, inferable views of an unapparent world, she told me, she wanted everything to happen at once, how we too easily submit to the tyranny of time. She did not want to watch the film, but wanted to have watched it, she did not want to read the book, she wanted to have read it, she did not want to do, but to have done, only then can she live how she wished to, with all experiences behind her, and to live outside time, where there is no more waiting, where there are no expectations.

Street Grain

Shatter blue cast textures, toxic Villager uneases shreds of lace lungs, anodyne light yellow pools pavements, burning soles with drenched feet pass hurriedly from fetid homes, working eyes darker, sleepless cell-grains, tapered in frictions.

There is no blank paper, she said.
This book of irresponsible texts.
Villager of hallucination can be observed.
Art for Pre-Enlightened atheists, art sans information.
For all images entropy is the subject.
Devour spectacle, perhaps even undeterred, lines of letters.

So from this rotting room, monochrome was the view of sunsets over the islands.

Stop Minding Lots

Breach grasping crania fallen breath behind ancillary stacks push grounded between edging streets incursive capillaries lack salient skin brought relapsed news for imbroglio places to such imbalanced pained pictures standing mile stones trip races towards towers of bastion creatures retrieving hanging from horn gates touching craven fingers receiving sequentials b b b belong to ivory gate day days laying filled readily dissuading torc turn torn apparent braying caned soil covered Saxon hand pairings unlicked ward shade broke wires between edible string crying chord beds transparent pebbles transplantable clouds pooling drawn crushed nettles win winter war posts around core tires where weight rushed stream grinding salt binding cot minding lots.

Landscape

Hoar grit cracked wind bitten tiles where evening light withdrew from the unopened house, the unrecognisable door was set amongst many doors of a trompe l'oeil wall, the figure sat beside a stone tree played games with alabaster rocks and dusty finger divots, a web of drying ivy trailed amongst the many petrified fauna capitalising walls about the square, on a calcified wooden bench I sat watching the figure at play and the puzzle of acid street light as it etched the corroding buildings, through calotype windows I saw shadowed paintings in ostentatious frames hanging in lavish rooms, yet perhaps these too were elaborate hoaxed apertures to an unsure house, I watched as the sun at length glanced a first glow onto a near distant rooftop, the figure lay down on the grimy ground and closed-eyed pulled a blanket of browning ivy across itself, the silhouette of a bird trapped within the nearby room drew in the night from along the street, untempered by webbed lamp illumination I stood with intent to determine some disagreeable nook to pass this over-misting day, just as an unsung door carelessly swung open, I knew then all that I feared and why ivy grows towards shadow.

Calafon

Lives crawl as melodic debris from shallow cracks, sallow skin forming ground to which dappled bodies fall wraps over the yellowing teeth and unpolished crania, words no longer able to drift away spiral and splinter about inhibited heads, engraved carrion hang beside each bed, here where once dread boats calmly drifted, pulsing amongst seeping posts, melt shadows bleach this remote beach, tied by whispers, damp from tedium, liquorice stained, these are the disengaged words of an uncompelled man, tracing journeys along a many bridged river, from a blasted revolution, cast-off cameras are discovered beside abandoned letters home, while navigable rivers narrow, those who live amongst the circus creatures of perishing wanderers, leave to wait underground until the caves of Deino, Enyo and Pemphredo reflect again moving images of Paris, better fed peasants lead the wheeled cadges along deserted boulevards, where pillared palaces are once-overed by an affray of unfunctional floorcloths, and children wait over-toyed in inaccessible gatehouses, rails run for the distribution of worthless statues, once scratched clean night-schools beat again at echoing sand courts, shouting and writhing over ledgers and copies of indiscernible illustrations, where demoted mothers are sewn into indivisible seams, autotrophs stand drooling outside, gagging before pylon arrangers and chess putti, who lose the hour pulling laden tables from the earth by snapping threads from within their ornate vaults, neighbours watching through slits in over-bricked walls blow heat across unborn teeth, blackened to grind moments into absurdly smaller moments, an image on previous era skin of pestilential furniture is polished to reflect not who but when, and outside the collector's house, diners have come to drink from the timid breath of their host slumped in the corner, as each gasps at the hollow room and bites into vacated mirrors, strung out mists of a hypnoreal up-light snap at the vast waves of reassembled architecture hovering above the well-roofed nests, an unecstatic sur-erratic plague of voices leaking from every joint unravels the decorous armies, which in turn fall from cloven cliffs of disintegrating books, and halting in the marsh, the unattended procession of tourniqueted janissaries stand dripping in the unattached rain, despondent at the nauseating sound of pages turning.

Beside the Wall

Stand beside the mirror and watch the waiter with painted cheeks grin at sitters fining beside the leaf-mould irons roasting effervescent spit, paper hands flutter about catching the snowy ash, light-blown figures walk into a wall of rain, an Autumn fall of fingers dissolve into the piano keys, eyes of the quiet open to listen to a great storm low about the lit chimneys, slo-mo rain thundering through the peristaltic village streets. The Pale Lady woke to the Opera of the Deluge, she said she was once lost on a beach, sea granules like greasy hair washing her calloused feet, as it did the calcareous cliffs. Morning depressions emulate silent adjuration, outside the riven land remote weather dashed amongst the flint layered house, on the stone shelf a cold cotton lamp flickering low beside the daubed terracotta bust animates its long vacated face, the woadwaxen book fell to the floor, the flayed door rattles, cackles of rain dampened the declining land, and night failed to open even the unsound window.

The Carcass of an Insufficient

Cross-country crowds, startling old crows and crying into their swarming soup, neglect an unhinged man, with his head in a box and grubby watch-the-bloodsucker lens he reaps a slice and sticks it to a glass, the stained images of a damp hundred dash interlines the pockets of the harlequins' ragged suits, where here in the parlour mixed 'n' masked jelly-beans, translucent automata, congeal in a cake tin, as a likeness in a locket, I knew a bloke who thought he'd lost a tanner, he lost five stone looking for it, up-shoot the weeping faces, down-shoot the gasping racers, catch waving hankies and flailing bleaters, with their distressed tapping and filial slapping, I knew a dog, an appalling smell, a bloke, who barked like a crow, an old crow, he threw away his chewed slippers, ripped corners from the bedsheet to wrap his toes, ate on Sundays, warmed his arse on Mondays, wasted his face on every other day, but for Wednesdays when he, she, bounced from the acid lampposts all the way to damnable home O'Clock, dreamt it was his pillow, 'er says, screaming on his pill-o, a pill-o, a rancid bed of will-o, fading from the street-o, until his name was whispered gone, in sleep under damp light walk the night stairs, then wake for a day of hay packing and gristle chewing. She saw him, draining pith, opening glug, glug windows for all to savour, and look there, gurgle gargoyle gag and gasp, sisters haggle, fighters rasp, to salivate is to culminate, outside Better Betties the grubby boy, pocketing worms, breeding germs, waited short trousered in slobbering rain for his Easter-Egg, bantering emptors battle with lardy and wobble-wheeled perambulators, I heard, she told me the price and I literally spit in my handbag, I listened, this man says he fills the scuttle in tweenies' rooms before off to mistress

Semele's for a dozen Kraters, so I ended up in bed, ferreting for a bloated bottle, fettling chips on vinegar blankets, a dead sleeper beside a dripping bucket, his brother tuned up, black coat, black trousers, black hat, white socks, a bloke on the radio said you can sell anything to anyone wearing white socks, Bandy Baker the bandage maker, he married a Welsh woman and moved to China, in Rummaging Street, in the tea strained house, beside the crusty bedside, odd couple, the vacuum plugged into the light socket, fight in the black and white dark, this is someone else's bag, you see, I'll wear the clothes and the shoes too small, nice shoes, all the same, you wait here, with your cheese- knife and your trousers, and I'll be back, shortly, so said the wife, taking a hankie from the peg, pursing it along with key, plug, and, as she's not so far though as a bus ticket, a waining coat. A last raid on the upper floor, clear this lot out then decorate, weren't you an actor, I was, broken by shared toilets, fancy skirting landladies and I didn't sound good in colour, you see, but for now, this room, and photographs of me in rags, which I pin to trees, with telephone tags, and hope someone sees, me, and knows what I will be, one up-and-gladdening day, the flower lady knew him, at home in an aviary, clowned for the best he did, ran bags of assorted twaddle past many a wobbling crowd, now how did it go, what he said he dreamt, I've got his old iron saucepans, here drying on the line, nicked they were by the fat bloke who moved into his larder, shame the elastic went, but the handles are still good though not attached to the pans, and now there is no one, holding the finish line, that is, waiting for the prattling old picaro to appear, as a peck somewhere along that distant path.

Height of a Postbox

Use old friends as old nails, insoluble machines, disfigured as leaves, falling as disinclined stairs, in the long gone moat house, where second cousins never meet, her words stick to the soles of torch bearers crawling between windblown lamplights hanging strip wired from the mottled walls, I called into the hill, a pneumatic voice paring scales from my sun chilled face, beckoning needle clad figures which swim between coastal arches, Etruscan jesters running from entangled periodicals stacked in tens, whereas Phoenicians hoard by sixties, here hangs the winter garlic and the horrisonant sounding-bell, detainers' faces leak insipid dribble into the populating sewer works, stitching dimes into the hems of drained amphorae before shipping to *Ultima Thule*, dull rings the hydro-saw, children tear at the hellebore, I suffer from an overstuffed bedstead, she wrote at a lean hour, waking nights all thoughts settle onto windy barks and wave at sepulchral cavalcades, steadily gouging the sludgy road, from the greying town into the inevitable unlit land. I remember when no one would listen, fumbling ears spoke into an absorbent shoulder, word-like voices ran down walls rancid and sticky, sighs of grinding poets grated the inner thighs of the hideous and injurious, epiphytes gather for sing-songs, the naked faces drawing water from a pipe bent-nailed to the daub wall, ere gales mock the pilgrims, devoutly kissing the pissing stone, clues to the end excrete from between the seams of senseless letters, pencilling in a collection of incidents that aren't true and searching for evidence to confirm the falsity, affairs are frames thrown into the sea, read the headstone, on Vida Street, and in the very long corridor quietly waiting is good enough, sewing ourselves to the floor, a core repudiation of a flimsy hat, she declared, and rasping cries seep from the teeth of those who do not flee, this is the wisdom of humanity.

South of Autumn

She talks behind her pillow as she walks, emptying her grief onto billowing sheets, tentered as they were without the ancient mossy walls, beyond the host of colourless figures who glide silently along unrecognised streets, she wandered amongst the standing marble crowd, stoic and unmoved, stripped of pigment, tepid to the caress, flickering in the light of the burning pedestalled statues. In a stained land, colonised and, condensed in places, disassembled by faces, inevitability poised, waiting with tongues, she looks to the fire to dampen the lips of those who yearn to drink from it. She will visit the lakes, with her pale lips and neglected stories, weathering the tender breezes, and walk amongst the long cooling towers set amongst the kind-fingered mountains, then wait amongst the machine of grass, a play of hair amongst a slipping sky, and with a brad ripped from a perishing plank she wrote on a rusting silo the sounds of those gasping images scratched of views from this side of the liminal.

The Institute of Incoherent Geography

Grains drag thoughts to petrifaction, the road squanders its linear gain in a mis-matching of signs, imitation of surety captures seamless requisites, down dream the spiral, down dream the precept of height, the spire from which guides a small door oversees this monochrome vista, unwired yet not unholed, the vengeful pen betrays hand and ink, make marks on yesterday's surface, over rubbing fingers being a trace of digital imperfections, blood on the rice leaves islands to cure before the neap waves, meat breath braves Neptunian solace, dogged wastrels belie a belief in under-nurtured parasites, as bedlam carries an architect's son to the tills of buried sand, the long walk being a rare night of calm, caresses the mote which flecks the call of a benefactor's cold kiss on the petulant's broken grimace, burden laced, the innocent hand re-strains the bone of the saint, a sceptical sigh to be kept amongst the unfixed pens, unbent paperclips, planetary marbles, interwoven marvels, a cauldron of dust and overwrought lust, baneful and overstated, compelled to apply fixity to an embryonic spectacle, an ambassador's vicissitude, a play on a musty wish, embraces all who esteem the caretaker's paperwork, notifying this pocket of participants that a penchant for overlooking the grasslands instigates the gate-full of insinuates to abate each calibration and dissolve the right to roam within gaps between stations, slow slides the tides, again the immaterial inland proffers an excessive blend of non-reflective chairs to re-twang the maxim, so quietly bows the beekeeper's daughter, where the vile orchard spawns the seed of further morality, an intercalation of gaseous contentment is placed, towards a further infliction of calculable divisions and inter-dormitory germination. High on long land hill along the gravel path the insoluble innocent forms beside the drifting fog, in the soft sun on a verdigris gate sits that beckoning figure, who in imagining, winds back all steps taken from the elegant tower towards that sweet brook.

Scuff Marks

When delusionary coupling becomes atonal background ash, hire due, one market, two waisting, arguing sleeves and aches and times to leave, a light is on and they are met by no one, climbing imprinted steps to blank stares and unmatched rooms. In a shaded room of books and a bed of sketches, unread notes to self on ripped corners of yellowing paper taped to the wall hang like desiccated skin, October as a *method* of being inexact, she said, the only month in which to precisely observe unsurety. There's no basement like my basement, bruised brick, walls dripping, ripple-stained stairs, chairs all tipping, fallacious light of an intemperate bulb, a phlegmatic air of mucous temperament, furniture you wouldn't stand a cat on, and a dense and grimy-grey ulcer of a window, I wait and I draw, inside no one listens, outside the days spoil.

I write knowing only mottled September light from a Georgian window softly glance across faintly dusted air and moth wing furniture. In a painfully redolent house I sit, to the musty quiet of a late afternoon, a sun quietly cracks to a lowing sky, and across the path seasoned leaves soberly dance to maundering breezes. I waken the brass lamp stand with a bakelite click, masking this corner of the blue evening with jaundiced intonation.

I greeted her in a language neither of us understood, in the fenced-off forest, bordered by this dry dirt lane which ends a mile or so at the bank leading down to the motorway, we walked behind each tree, to see if the tallow lanterns were lit in the small homes fitting hopelessly in the sore holes, then standing at the fence, we wondered at the vast over varnished skyscape of impasto clouds over scumbled hues boiling above the undernourished valley of silting streams, straying crops, truncated houses and dead-headed tracks.

Passing on

She is what light is for, beyond surety, hurt, melody and precision, she knows my name, when I was once like her, she yells the word in frank joy, carefully crawling across to my crooked smile, she calls me by what I once was, young, ignorant, futureless, focussed and unsound, soon she may call me what I am, a land of sludgy thought and swelling bile, a despairing help, a failing word, unable to give enough, indeed, unchanged a whole life through, though uniquely failing to live forever.

Discoloured

I sat on the put-me-up, fags in plastic bag, whisky in paper cup, a monotone drone between these sloping walls, affliction is stronger here than companionship, this is the call of the vile, you see, the irreducible centre, a slow grow crack in the innermost wall, how the warm night seeps in, neon strips above the highway, welcome after welcome, those aren't just place names stuck up on those signposts, you know, they are leased towns, crammed with leaking existence, she told me she was beside the lake, in which all the cattle were drowned, the rain stank, the colours weren't colours but a million prattling whispers, and my heart a rusty oldcam ground on, we all need a fingerpost to prod us, I'd walked back along yellow snowed streets to the house, I scraped my shitty boots on the cracked edge of the remaining path, turned the squealing handle on a deadlock door and stepped into the dim hall, I couldn't find the stairs, the walking about on the countless upper floors echoed down though the boarded up landings, I crossed to one of the streaming doors and through the grimy glass counted the ashen faces being fed tea from sooty cups and corner cakes from liverish plates, not as many as once were, they fear to look out now onto the surviving street and watch the remaining few touch each other's fingertips as they pass. In my room I can count, ninety-nine-nine, thirty-seven-ten, six-six, forty-twenty-one, this isn't counting, you see, what's the inference, better words aren't in order, you see, meaning drifts off to a better place, like Chekhov's vast, lingering three page novels, the bed squeals as if I'd laid down on a rat, the blankets crawled up over my graceless form and scratched me softly to a congested, infested sleep.

www.ingramcontent.com/pod-product-compliance
Lightning Source LLC
Chambersburg PA
CBHW031929080426
42734CB00007B/613